Questions and Answers: Countries

Russia

by Kremena Spengler

Consultant:
Nancy S. Kollmann, Director
Center for Russian, East European, and Eurasian Studies
Stanford University
Stanford, California

Capstone
press

Mankato, Minnesota

Fact Finders is published by Capstone Press
151 Good Counsel Drive, P.O. Box 669, Mankato, Minnesota 56002
www.capstonepress.com

Library of Congress Cataloging-in-Publication Data
Spengler, Kremena.
    Russia / by Kremena Spengler.
    p. cm.—(Fact finders. Questions and answers: Countries)
    Includes bibliographical references and index.
    Contents: Where is Russia?—When did Russia become a country?—What type of
government does Russia have?—What kind of housing does Russia have?—What are
Russia's forms of transportation?—What are Russia's major industries?—What is school
like in Russia?—What are Russia's favorite sports and games?—What are the traditional
art forms in Russia?—What major holidays do people in Russia celebrate?—What are the
traditional foods in Russia?—What is family life like in Russia?
    ISBN 0-7368-2692-0 (hardcover)
    1. Russia (Federation)—Juvenile literature. [1. Russia (Federation)] I. Title. II. Series.
DK510.23.S69 2005
947—dc22   2003026879

Editorial Credits
Megan Schoeneberger, editor; Kia Adams, series designer; Jennifer Bergstrom, book
    designer; maps.com, map illustrator; Wanda Winch, photo researcher; Scott Thoms,
    photo editor; Eric Kudalis, product planning editor

Photo Credits
Bruce Coleman Inc./Bill Foley, 7; Corbis/AFP, 15, 19; Corbis/Diego Lezama Orezzoli,
12; Corbis/Reuters NewMedia Inc., 23; Corbis/Reuters NewMedia Inc./POOL/Misha
Japaridze, 8; Corbis/Royalty-Free, 1; Corbis/Wally McNamee, 10–11; Corbis/Wolfgang
Kaehler, cover (foreground); Corel, cover (background); Cory Langley, 21; Eileen R.
Herrling, 4; Getty Images Inc./Ian Walton, 9; StockHaus Limited, 29 (bottom); Svetlana
Zhurkina, 25, 27, 29 (top); UNICORN Stock Photos/MRP/Jeff Greenberg, 17; Wolfgang
Kaehler, 13

Artistic Effects
Photodisc/C Squared Studios, 24; Photodisc/Don Tremain, 18

1 2 3 4 5 6 09 08 07 06 05 04

Table of Contents

Features

Where is Russia?

Russia is a country in Europe and Asia. It is almost twice as large as the United States.

Parts of Russia are flat. Cold plains called **tundra** lie in northern Russia. South of the tundra are forests called **taiga**. Grasslands lie south of the taiga.

Mountains and forests cover much of Russia. ▶

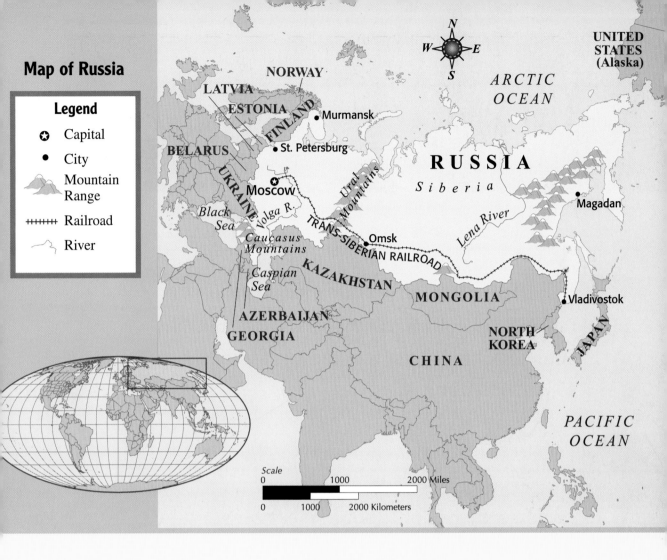

Map of Russia

Legend

⊗ Capital

● City

Mountain Range

++++++ Railroad

River

Russia's landforms include mountains. Russia has two large mountain ranges. The Caucasus Mountains are in the southwest. The Ural Mountains divide western Russia from eastern Russia, or Siberia. Mountains also cover Russia's eastern coast.

5

When did Russia become a country?

Russia became its own country on August 24, 1991. Since 1917, Russia had been part of the **Union** of Soviet Socialist **Republics** (U.S.S.R.). The U.S.S.R. was also known as the Soviet Union. Russia was the largest of the 15 Soviet republics.

The Soviet Union had a communist government. Under **communism**, houses, land, and factories belonged to the government. The people were meant to share everything.

Fact!

Boris Yeltsin was the first president of Russia after the end of the Soviet Union.

Paintings and statues of communist leaders were common in the Soviet Union.

The Soviet Union's government did not treat people fairly. They were not free. The republics wanted more power. In September 1991, the republics ended communism and the Soviet Union. Each republic, including Russia, became its own country.

What type of government does Russia have?

Russia is a federation. A federation is a group of states joined together with a single government. Each state has its own government.

Russians elect a president. The president makes important decisions. The president also chooses a group of leaders. These leaders help run the government.

Vladimir Putin became Russia's president in 1999. ➤

The Kremlin in Moscow is the meeting place of Russia's government.

Russia also has a **parliament**. The parliament votes on laws suggested by the president. The parliament has two groups called houses. Leaders of Russia's states choose the members of the upper house. The Russian people elect the members of the lower house.

What kind of housing does Russia have?

In Russian cities, houses are not common. Most Russians live in large apartment buildings. Most people have small apartments. These apartments often have a kitchen, a bathroom, and one or two other rooms.

Where do people in Russia live?

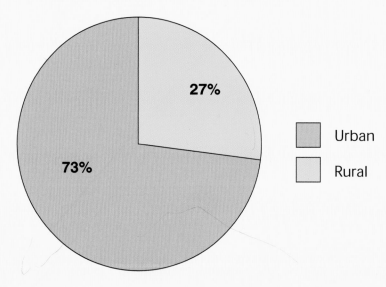

27%

73%

Urban

Rural

Many Russians decorate the walls of their rooms with colorful rugs.

Many city people also have small country houses called dachas. They grow vegetables and fruit outside these houses.

Russians in the country live in farmhouses. Some of these houses are larger than apartments. Few farmhouses have running water or indoor toilets.

What are Russia's forms of transportation?

Russians use public transportation in cities. They ride buses, streetcars, or subways. Car travel is less popular in Russia than in some other countries. Many Russians cannot afford cars. Roads are old and bumpy.

Streetcars are common in Russian cities. ▶

The Trans-Siberian Railroad is about 5,600 miles (9,000 kilometers) long.

Railroads carry most of Russia's goods. The Trans-Siberian Railroad is a long railroad between Moscow and Vladivostok.

Many ships sail from Russia's **ports**. They also travel on rivers and canals before these waterways freeze in winter.

What are Russia's major industries?

Many **industries** make up Russia's **economy**. Factories make steel, cars, planes, ships, and farm vehicles. Russia's spacecraft industry is world famous.

Russia is rich in oil, natural gas, metals, and wood. Workers use these **natural resources** to make machines and other goods. Russia also sells these products to other countries.

What does Russia import and export?	
Imports	**Exports**
consumer goods	natural gas
machinery	petroleum
medicine	wood and wood products

Russians drill for oil in the Pacific Ocean.

Farming is a small industry in Russia. Only about one-tenth of the land is good for farming. Wheat, **barley**, potatoes, and beets grow in southern Russia.

What is school like in Russia?

School begins on September 1 and ends in late May. In lower grades, one teacher teaches all subjects. Russian students go through school with the same group of classmates. They usually sit at desks built for two. They make close friends with other students in the group.

Fact!

Russian schools need more teachers. In the 1990s, many teachers left to find higher paying jobs.

Russian students often share a desk with a classmate.

Most Russian children start school at age 6 or 7. Students must complete ninth grade. After ninth grade, most students choose to finish 10th and 11th grade. Other students choose to go to trade schools to train for a job.

What are Russia's favorite sports and games?

Russia's cold weather makes winter sports popular. Favorite winter sports are hockey, ice-skating, and cross-country skiing. Russian teams in these sports have won many medals in world contests.

Russians also play summer sports. The most popular summer sport is soccer. Other favorites are gymnastics, track and field, swimming, and fishing.

Fact!

More than 300 Russian hockey players have played in North America's National Hockey League.

Ice-skating is a popular sport in Russia.

Russians enjoy playing chess. Adults and children play this board game at home, in clubs, or in parks. Most world chess champions are from Russia.

What are the traditional art forms in Russia?

Russian music and dance are popular in many countries. Composer Sergei Prokofiev wrote *Peter and the Wolf*. This piece uses music to tell a story. Different musical instruments are used for each animal and person in the story. Pyotr Tchaikovsky wrote the music for *The Nutcracker* ballet. Russian ballet dancers are known for their grace and skill. Famous dancers from Russia include Mikhail Baryshnikov and Rudolf Nureyev.

Fact!

Russians make pictures of saints called icons. Icons usually are painted on wood. They hang in churches and homes.

Large nesting dolls have smaller dolls that fit inside them.

Russians make art objects from wood.
They paint wooden boxes with scenes from
folktales. Wooden nesting dolls are famous art
items. These brightly painted dolls fit inside
each other.

What major holidays do people in Russia celebrate?

New Year is the biggest holiday in Russia. Russians decorate a fir tree, eat a large meal, and give gifts. Children believe that gifts come from Grandfather Frost. He comes with his granddaughter, the Snow Maiden. They travel in a sled pulled by three horses.

What other holidays do people in Russia celebrate?

Day of the Russian Federation State Flag
Independence Day
International Women's Day
Spring and Labor Holiday

People march in parades to celebrate Victory Day.

On May 9, Russians celebrate Victory Day. This holiday marks the Russian victory over Germany in World War II (1939–1945). People who fought in the war gather in parks and town squares. They wear their medals. They lay flowers at war monuments.

What are the traditional foods of Russia?

Russian meals usually have a main dish. Meat-filled dumplings are a common main dish. Another popular dish is blini. These thin pancakes are topped with sour cream and butter or jam.

Russian dishes often mix meat and vegetables, especially potatoes. Borscht is a Russian soup. It has red beets, potatoes, meat, and cabbage. Russians often top borscht with sour cream.

Fact!

In summer and early fall, many Russians pick mushrooms in forests. People dry or can them for winter.

Meat and potatoes are common in Russian meals.

Russian meals often start with snacks. One popular snack is salty fish eggs called caviar. Other snacks are herring, pickled mushrooms, and sliced meats. Russians serve bread with every meal.

What is family life like in Russia?

Russian families often have only one or two children. Many grandparents live with the families. They help raise the children.

In Russia, both parents usually work. Many adults take extra jobs to pay the bills. While parents are at work, most small children go to preschool.

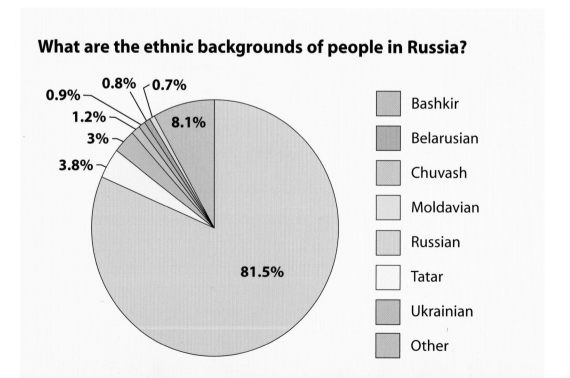

What are the ethnic backgrounds of people in Russia?

0.9%
0.8%
0.7%
1.2%
3%
3.8%
8.1%
81.5%

- Bashkir
- Belarusian
- Chuvash
- Moldavian
- Russian
- Tatar
- Ukrainian
- Other

Russian grandparents often help care for their grandchildren.

In their spare time, Russians welcome friends to their homes. They share their best food with guests. Few Russians have enough money to eat in restaurants.

Russia Fast Facts

Official name:

Russian Federation

Land area:

6,562,085 square miles
(16,995,800 square kilometers)

Average annual precipitation:

20 inches (51 centimeters)

Average January temperature:

21 degrees Fahrenheit
(minus 6 degrees Celsius)

Average July temperature:

71 degrees Fahrenheit
(22 degrees Celsius)

Population:

144,526,278 people

Capital city:

Moscow

Language:

Russian

Natural resources:

coal, iron ore, natural
gas, petroleum

Religions:

Russian Orthodox	75%
Islamic	19%
Other	6%

Money and Flag

Money:

Russian money is called the ruble. One ruble equals 100 kopecks. In 2004, 1 U.S. dollar equaled 28.5 rubles. One Canadian dollar equaled 21.7 rubles.

Flag:

The Russian flag has equal horizontal stripes of white, blue, and red. Russia has used the flag since 1991.

Learn to Speak Russian

The Russian language uses a different alphabet than the English language. This Cyrillic (suh-RIHL-ik) alphabet has 33 letters. Here are some Russian words using the English alphabet.

English	Russian	Pronunciation
hello	privyet	(pri-VYET)
good-bye	dosvidanya	(dah-svee-DAH-nyah)
please	pozhaluista	(poh-JAH-lahs-tah)
thank you	spasibo	(spah-SEE-bah)
yes	da	(DAH)
no	nyet	(NYET)

Glossary

barley (BAR-lee)—a common type of grain; grains are the seeds of a cereal plant.

communism (KOM-yuh-niz-uhm)—a way of organizing a country so that all the land, houses, and factories belong to the government, and the profits are shared by all

economy (i-KON-uh-mee)—the way a country runs its industry, trade, and finance

industry (IN-duh-stree)—a single branch of business or trade

natural resource (NACH-ur-uhl REE-sorss)—a material found in nature that is useful to people

parliament (PAR-luh-muhnt)—the group of people who have been elected to make laws in some countries

port (PORT)—a harbor or place where boats and ships can dock or anchor safely

republic (ree-PUHB-lik)—one of the political units that made up the Soviet Union

taiga (TYE-guh)—a forest with mainly pine trees

tundra (TUHN-druh)—a cold area where trees do not grow; the soil under the ground in the tundra is permanently frozen.

union (YOON-yuhn)—two or more things or people joined together to form a larger group

Internet Sites

FactHound offers a safe, fun way to find Internet sites related to this book. All of the sites on FactHound have been researched by our staff.

Here's how:
1. Visit *www.facthound.com*
2. Type in this special code **0736826920** for age-appropriate sites. Or enter a search word related to this book for a more general search.
3. Click on the **Fetch It** button.

FactHound will fetch the best sites for you!

Read More

Allan, Tony. *The Russian Revolution.* 20th-Century Perspectives. Chicago: Heinemann Library, 2003.

De Capua, Sarah. *Russia.* Discovering Cultures. New York: Benchmark Books, 2003.

Kort, Michael. *Russia.* Nations in Transition. New York: Facts on File, 2004.

Ransome, Galya. *Russia.* The Changing Face Of. Chicago: Raintree, 2004.

Index